CW01460890

Original title:
Snowfall Peace

Author: Mirell Mesipuu
ISBN HARDBACK: 978-9908-1-1594-8
ISBN PAPERBACK: 978-9908-1-1595-5
ISBN EBOOK: 978-9908-1-1596-2

Serenity Wrapped in Frost

Soft flakes dance in gentle air,
Twinkling lights, a magic flair.
Laughter echoes, hearts embrace,
Winter's charm in every space.

Warm fires crackle, stories shared,
Joyful moments, love declared.
Mugs of cocoa, sweet delight,
Together we spark the night.

Alpine Silhouettes at Dusk

Mountains stand in twilight's glow,
Whispers of the winds that blow.
Candles flicker, shadows play,
Nature's canvas at the end of day.

Stars emerge in velvet skies,
Promises of joy arise.
Snowflakes swirl in frosty dance,
In this moment, we find our chance.

Traces of Tranquility

The world slows down beneath the moon,
Silent nights hum a soft tune.
Footprints linger on the ground,
In this stillness, peace is found.

Crisp air wraps like a gentle hug,
Nature's beauty, a soothing drug.
Hearts are light, worries fade,
In harmony, memories are made.

The Winter's Gift of Stillness

Blankets of white, soft and pure,
A pause in life, an embrace secure.
Gentle moments, a time to rest,
In winter's arms, we are blessed.

Frosty breath swirls as we skate,
In every smile, warmth does await.
Crafting dreams with every sigh,
Underneath the starry sky.

The Soft Nestle of White

In the forest, snowflakes dance,
A twirl of joy in winter's glance.
Blankets cover the ground so bright,
A soft nestle of purest white.

Children laughing, faces aglow,
Building snowmen, hearts full of flow.
With every flake, a story unfolds,
In the warmth of the season, love never grows old.

Enveloping Stillness

The world is hushed, a gentle sigh,
As stars twinkle in the midnight sky.
Moonbeams cast their soft embrace,
In this stillness, we find our place.

Crisp air whispers, a sweet caress,
Nature's palette in snowy dress.
Footprints trace a path through night,
In the silence, all feels right.

Winter's Quiet Melody

Hear the whispers of the trees,
They sing softly with the breeze.
Crystals glisten on every branch,
In this moment, we take a chance.

Voices carry through the air,
Laughter mingles everywhere.
Hot cocoa warms our hands in cheer,
Winter's melody, crystal clear.

A Cloak of Tranquility

Wrapped in warmth, we gather near,
With family, friends, all we hold dear.
A soft cloak of tranquility,
In every heart, joy's sweet decree.

Fires crackle, embers glow bright,
As we share stories through the night.
Together we dance in winter's grace,
In this moment, we've found our place.

Snowbound Serenity

The snowflakes dance in twilight's glow,
Soft whispers weave through the world below.
Each flake a star, a story to tell,
In winter's embrace, all is well.

Children laugh under a frosty sky,
Building dreams where the snowmen lie.
Laughter echoes, pure delight,
In this snowbound serenity, hearts take flight.

Celestial Silence

The moon hangs bright, a silver crest,
Wrapped in stars, the night is blessed.
Gentle breezes brush the trees,
In celestial silence, the world finds ease.

Soft shadows dance on the quiet ground,
In this moment, peace is found.
Crickets sing their evening song,
In harmony where dreams belong.

Nature's Soft Shield

Beneath the canopy, magic lies,
Whispers of nature, a soft surprise.
Leaves caress the ground in gold,
A tapestry of stories untold.

Gentle creatures roam with grace,
In the forest's heart, a sacred place.
Where every rustle, every sigh,
Creates a world where spirits fly.

An Evening of Stillness

The sun dips low with a fiery hue,
Casting shadows where the children grew.
Crickets chirp their soothing tune,
In an evening of stillness, beneath the moon.

Lanterns flicker with a warm embrace,
Gathered friends share laughter's grace.
In this moment, time stands still,
Hearts are light, and dreams fulfill.

The Silence between Crystals

The snowflakes dance in playful flight,
Each crystal sparkles, pure and bright.
In the hush of winter, laughter sings,
As joy and magic softly springs.

Beneath the moon, the world aglow,
Whispers of dreams in twilight's flow.
Nature's canvas, white and clear,
A festive spirit lingers near.

Beauty in the Cold

Icicles hang like nature's art,
Each glimmer strikes a warming heart.
Laughter mingles with chilly air,
As voices blend in winter's fair.

Around the fire, stories unfold,
Frosty nights wrapped in tales retold.
With mugs of cocoa, friends unite,
In this beauty, warmth feels right.

Muffled Echoes

Footsteps crunch on a snowy lane,
Echoes of joy, a sweet refrain.
Fires crackle with glowing cheer,
As the festive spirit draws near.

Children's laughter fills the night,
Chasing shadows, hearts are light.
A symphony of warmth and sound,
In muffled echoes, joy is found.

A Palette of White

Blankets of snow, soft and wide,
Where winter's magic does abide.
Lights twinkle on the frosty trees,
Dancing to the whispering breeze.

Gathered close, we share the feast,
In this wonder, we are released.
A palette of white, pure delight,
The festive season feels just right.

The Breath of Frost

The frost kisses the ground below,
As laughter dances in the air,
Lights twinkle in the twilight glow,
A merry warmth beyond compare.

Chill whispers call the revelers near,
With cups raised high in joyful cheers,
Each heart ignites, the festive cheer,
Resonates as the new year nears.

Candles flicker, casting glows,
On faces bright with pure delight,
The spirit of the season flows,
Embracing all in the starry night.

In this dance of frost and cheer,
We celebrate with carefree hearts,
For every laugh and every tear,
A cherished song as joy imparts.

Crystal Moments

Crystal bells echo in the breeze,
Glistening like the stars so bright,
Moments frozen, hearts at ease,
As joy rushes through the night.

Children's laughter fills the air,
While snowflakes twirl with every leap,
With friends and family everywhere,
Creating memories we shall keep.

Warmth wraps us like a gentle hug,
As stories are shared by the fire,
Each glance, each smile, an endless tug,
Binding us in love's pure choir.

In crystal moments, time stands still,
Embraced by joy, we feel so free,
With every song, we feel the thrill,
Of life's sweet dance, eternally.

White Veils of Quietude

White veils drift down, a soft embrace,
Each flake whispers a tale untold,
Nature cloaked in velvet grace,
A peaceful hush, a sight to behold.

Beneath the moon's silvery light,
Families gather close and near,
Wrapped in warmth, hearts take flight,
Creating bonds as winter's cheer.

Candles flicker, casting dreams,
In this tranquil, snowy delight,
With laughter mingling in gentle streams,
Our spirits soar, our fears take flight.

In white veils of quietude we find,
A moment's pause, a sacred thread,
Ties of love that gently bind,
As the season whispers, joy is spread.

The Peaceful Descent

The gentle snow begins to fall,
A soft descent, a dreamlike state,
Nature whispers, a tranquil call,
In the silence, we contemplate.

Children gather with hopeful eyes,
Building snowmen with laughter bright,
As echoes of joy softly rise,
Transforming day into a night filled with light.

Families feast, the table spread,
With love and warmth wrapped in each bite,
As stories linger, fondly said,
Creating warmth on winter's night.

In this peaceful descent, we see,
The magic of the season unfold,
As hearts connect, wild and free,
Celebrating love, forever bold.

Celestial Stillness

Under the stars, the laughter flows,
Candles flicker, a warm glow shows.
In this night, hearts dance in glee,
Magic swirls, wild and free.

Joyous songs fill the crisp air,
Whispers of dreams, a festive flair.
Laughter and love, a tapestry spun,
Together we shine, united as one.

The moon laughs down, a silver thread,
In this moment, all worries shed.
With every twinkle, our spirits rise,
In celestial stillness, joy never dies.

Chasing Shadows in White

Snowflakes dance, a soft embrace,
Children giggle, pure delight on their face.
Joy abounds in this frozen world,
As laughter and cheer are freely unfurled.

Footprints trail through the glimmering white,
Chasing shadows under soft moonlight.
Every twirl, a story told,
In this winter wonderland, bright and bold.

Hot cocoa warms hands, a sweet, rich taste,
With every sip, no moment to waste.
As spirits rise, we cherish the night,
In chasing shadows, everything feels right.

Time Suspended in Frost

Time stands still in the frosty air,
As snow-covered branches take us there.
Moments linger, wrapped in a dream,
In winter's embrace, all hearts beam.

Glittering lights twinkle above,
Filling the night with warmth and love.
Laughter echoes, a symphony bright,
In this magic, everything feels light.

An orchestra of joy, the world in awe,
As families gather, time's gentle draw.
Each glance shared, a treasure to keep,
In this festive moment, our hearts leap.

The Art of Winter

Brushed with white, the landscape glows,
Nature's canvas in soft repose.
Fires crackle, filling the room,
As hearts expand, casting away gloom.

Sipping cider, wrapped in warmth,
Joyful tales of winter's charm.
Every laughter, a stroke of cheer,
Creating memories that hold us near.

Through frosted windows, we gaze outside,
At painted wonders, our hearts open wide.
In the art of winter, love is our guide,
Uniting us all, with spirits untied.

Frosty Reverie

Snowflakes twirl in playful glee,
Children laugh beneath the tree.
Lights aglow in colors bright,
Magic whispers through the night.

Hot cocoa warms our chilly hands,
Joyous hearts in winter lands.
Fireplace crackles, stories shared,
Glowing warmth, a love declared.

The world aglow, a soft embrace,
Every moment, a cherished space.
Glistening paths invite our feet,
In frosty reverie, life feels sweet.

So let the snow fall down like dreams,
And join in laughter, as it seems.
Together we'll dance, the night is young,
In a frosty world where songs are sung.

The Silence of Falling

Softly now the snow descends,
Whispers heard as daylight ends.
Blankets white on every street,
Nature's hush, a soothing beat.

Families gather, stories flow,
The warmth of love begins to grow.
Candles flicker, shadows play,
In the silence of this holiday.

A world transformed, so pure, so bright,
Stars above begin their flight.
Hearts align in tranquil peace,
The silent night brings sweet release.

As snowflakes dance in moonlit skies,
Laughter echoes, and spirits rise.
Together wrapped in warmth and cheer,
In the silence, joy draws near.

Ethereal Winter's Dance

Moonlight casts a silver glow,
In the twilight, magic flows.
Whirling leaves and twirling snow,
Ethereal dreams in winter's show.

Glittering frost on branches bare,
Entwined in wonder, we lay care.
Footsteps crunch on blankets white,
Chasing shadows in the night.

Stars above with twinkling eyes,
Invite our hearts to softly rise.
In this dance of cold and light,
Winter whispers, pure delight.

Join the swirl, the world is fair,
In this moment, love's in the air.
Hold me close, let's take the chance,
In the bliss of winter's dance.

Serenity in Crystal

Sparkling flakes on window panes,
Each a story, sweet refrains.
In tranquil spaces, time stands still,
Serenity sings a gentle thrill.

Icicles hang like crystal chimes,
Echoes soft of winter's rhymes.
A canvas blank, a wish renewed,
The peace of snow, the heart imbued.

Carols drift on frosty air,
Moments cherished, love laid bare.
Beneath the stars, we find our way,
In serenity, we long to stay.

So let the world slow down its pace,
In winter's arms, we find our grace.
Together in this frozen bliss,
A crystal world, a timeless kiss.

The Calm Before the Chill

The lights are strung with care,
Laughter dances in the air,
Warmth seeps through every heart,
As festive cheer begins to start.

Mugs of cocoa in our hands,
Glimmers twinkle, oh so grand,
Echoes of joy fill the night,
In this moment, pure delight.

Candles flicker, soft and bright,
Shadows play in winter's light,
Gather close, the warmth we share,
In this calm, we breathe the prayer.

The world awaits the snowflakes' fall,
But for now, we're having a ball,
With whispered dreams and soft embrace,
We'll hold this joy in time and space.

Stillness in the Flurry

Snowflakes glide, a gentle sway,
As laughter echoes, bright and gay,
In the hush, we find our glee,
While winter wraps us lovingly.

Children's giggles fill the park,
Creating warmth against the dark,
Every heart is light and free,
In this stillness, joy's decree.

Scarves are wrapped, the world a dream,
Together we share sweet cream,
With every snowball, every cheer,
The festivity draws us near.

In the night, the stars align,
With each connection, love will shine,
The flurry swirls, but we stand still,
In this wonder, hearts can fill.

Gentle Veil of Silence

Underneath the starry dome,
A quiet hush, a feeling home,
Snowy blankets grace the ground,
In this silence, joy is found.

The world is painted pure and white,
Soft whispers echo through the night,
With every breath, we find our peace,
In gentle moments, worries cease.

Nature stills, a tranquil song,
Reminding us where we belong,
With family gathered, hearts entwined,
In this veil, a love defined.

So let the winter winds now blow,
We hold each other, warmth will grow,
For in the silence, deep and wide,
Our festive spirit will abide.

Crystal Dreams Beneath Grey Skies

Grey clouds blanket the horizon seen,
Yet within, a festive sheen,
Crystal dreams sparkle and glow,
Through winter's charm, our spirits flow.

We gather round with stories told,
In cozy corners, hearts unfold,
Each memory woven with delight,
Beneath these skies, our spirits ignite.

The laughter roars like a joyful breeze,
While branches sway beneath the trees,
In every glance, a twinkling star,
Reminds us of how blessed we are.

So let the grey skies softly weep,
As we embrace this joy so deep,
Together, we create a song,
In crystal dreams, where we belong.

Crystal Quietude

In the snow a soft glow shines,
Wonders wrapped in quiet vines.
Laughter dances in the air,
Joyful hearts, a lively flare.

Candles flicker, warm and bright,
Whispers fill the starry night.
Chasing shadows, dreams take flight,
In this magic, pure delight.

Gifts of kindness, shared with grace,
Smiles emerge on every face.
Snowflakes twirl like gentle cheers,
Creating memories for the years.

Harmonies of joy resound,
In this festive love we're found.
Each moment, sweet and divine,
In crystal quietude we shine.

Frosted Dreams

Underneath the frosty moon,
Softly sings a winter tune.
Dreams wrapped up in snowflakes' care,
Floating down, a wishful prayer.

Lights aglow on every street,
Neighbors gather, voices sweet.
In the warmth of laughter shared,
Every heart is lightly bared.

Sipping cocoa, tales unfold,
Adventures new and memories old.
Families knit in cozy seams,
Woven tight in frosted dreams.

As the stars begin to gleam,
Hope ignites like a bright beam.
Together, we embrace the night,
In this season, pure delight.

Hushed Reflections

Amidst the glow of silver trees,
Time stands still upon the breeze.
Moments captured, softly glowed,
In hushed reflections, love bestowed.

Carols echo through the chill,
Every note a gentle thrill.
Gather round, the fire's light,
Hearts alight on this calm night.

Woven tales of those we hold,
Whispered close, a bond of gold.
In the stillness, hopes arise,
As we gaze into the skies.

Every sparkle brings a smile,
In this stillness, rest a while.
Joy persists in every glance,
In hushed reflections, hearts will dance.

The Stillness Within

While the world drifts into sleep,
Stars awaken, secrets keep.
In the stillness, peace descends,
A quiet magic, joy extends.

Snowflakes twirl like soft ballet,
Whispered dreams on pillows play.
Moments shared beside the fire,
Fueled by warmth, our hearts aspire.

With each laugh, the spirits rise,
Echoing in winter's skies.
Love unwrapped, a gift divine,
In this stillness, our hearts shine.

As the night softly unfolds,
Stories of our lives retold.
In the calm, we find our kin,
In the stillness, joy begins.

Muffled Moments

In the glow of twinkling lights,
Laughter dances through the nights.
Chirping songs of joy surround,
In this warmth, a peace is found.

Presents wrapped in colors bright,
Exchanging gifts, hearts feel light.
Joy spills forth like bubbles high,
Underneath the frost-kissed sky.

Candles flicker, shadows play,
Whispers of the festive day.
Gathered close, our spirits soar,
Moments cherished, evermore.

As snowflakes fall, we twirl and sway,
In this magic, let us stay.
Together, we embrace the cheer,
Muffled moments, held so dear.

Imagery of Silence

Stars hang low like dreams untold,
Covered blankets, warmth unfolds.
Silent nights with hearts ablaze,
In this stillness, joy conveys.

Footprints crunching on the snow,
Hints of laughter softly flow.
Every shadow glimmers bright,
In the tapestry of night.

Mugs of cocoa, steam ascends,
Sharing tales with all our friends.
Glistening lights on every tree,
In this silence, we feel free.

Magic whispers in the air,
Festive spirits everywhere.
Imagery of peace so grand,
Holds us close, hand in hand.

A Quiet Tapestry

Threaded moments, joy entwined,
Gentle echoes, hearts aligned.
Softly sung, a carol sweet,
In the quiet, life's complete.

Woven laughter, stories bright,
Embers dancing in the night.
Colors blend, a vibrant hue,
In this tapestry, me and you.

Candles casting gentle beams,
Sparkling hopes and whispered dreams.
With each smile that's shared anew,
Threads of love will carry through.

Underneath the blanket's sway,
We turn night into a play.
In these dreams, we find our fate,
A quiet tapestry, first-rate.

Beneath the Blanket

Beneath the blanket, cozy tight,
The world outside is pure delight.
Laughter peals like chimes of gold,
In this warmth, the tales unfold.

Frosty windows, patterns lace,
Captured moments, time and space.
Sipping cider, flavors merge,
In this stillness, hearts surge.

Children's giggles fill the air,
With each story, love lays bare.
As we gather round the flame,
Festive shadows call our name.

Magic twinkles, eyes alight,
Holding close this cherished night.
Beneath the blanket, dreams will sing,
In joy's embrace, our spirits cling.

Frosted Gardens of Reflection

In gardens frosted, joy takes flight,
With laughter dancing, hearts so bright.
Stars shimmering on petals fair,
Whispers of solace fill the air.

Colors burst in winter's embrace,
As warm fires glow, we share this space.
Glistening paths of pure delight,
Every moment feels just right.

Children's laughter, sweet and clear,
Brings forth cheer with loved ones near.
Marshmallow clouds in skies of blue,
Wrap our dreams in magic too.

So raise your glass to joy anew,
In frosted gardens, bright and true.
Where memories bloom, and spirits sing,
Embrace the peace that winter brings.

Crystal Silence in the Night

Underneath the crystal moon,
Silence wraps the night in tune.
Stars aglow, like diamonds shine,
Magic lingers, pure, divine.

Winter's chill, a tender sigh,
As whispers of soft dreams float by.
Frosted branches, nature's art,
We gather closely, hearts apart.

In the stillness, we find cheer,
A moment shared with ones held dear.
Echoes of laughter, warmth, and grace,
In this serene, enchanted space.

So let us bask in cozy glow,
With tales of joy in whispers low.
In crystal silence, let love flow,
As night enfolds us, soft and slow.

Quietude in the Drift

Amid the snow, a quiet drift,
Where spirit dances, hearts uplift.
Footprints mark the blank canvas,
Each step a story, warm and vast.

Gentle breaths of winter air,
Wrap us close, a tender care.
In solitude, yet not alone,
Friendship mirrors in the grown.

Fires crackle, flickering light,
We share our stories through the night.
Blankets woven with tales of yore,
Embrace the warmth, forevermore.

In quietude, let laughter ring,
For every heart has warmth to bring.
In the drift, we find our way,
To celebrate this joyful day.

Moonlit Whispers on White Fields

Moonlit whispers on white fields play,
As shadows dance and softly sway.
Each breath of night, a soothing balm,
Wrapped in peace, a tranquil calm.

Snowflakes twinkle, stars collide,
Together in this joyful ride.
The world aglow in silvery light,
Filling hearts with pure delight.

We gather close, our voices blend,
A melody of love to send.
Every glance and every smile,
Makes frosty moments worth the while.

So let us wander hand in hand,
In moonlight's glow, our dreams expand.
For in this night, together we weave,
The festive spirit, we believe.

Winter's Gentle Whispers

Snowflakes dance in the air,
Laughter echoes everywhere.
A carpet soft, and pure as white,
Joy ignites the chilly night.

Candles flicker, warmth in glow,
Gifts wrapped tightly, love will flow.
Families gather, stories shared,
Hearts united, none impaired.

Chiming bells ring through the street,
Children's footsteps, quick and fleet.
Sipping cocoa, cheeks aglow,
Winter's magic, all do know.

Stars above, a twinkling show,
Nature's beauty, just like so.
With each whisper, hope takes flight,
In this festive, cozy night.

Still Waters in the Frost

Silent beams of moonlit sheen,
Reflecting beauty, calm and serene.
Frosty trees in a ghostly white,
Nature's wonders, a true delight.

Whispers of joy on the crisp air,
Friends unite with love to share.
Gliding skates upon the ice,
Each joyful laugh, a sweet slice.

The world is wrapped in a soft embrace,
Time slows down, a gentle pace.
Hot spiced drinks, the warmth invites,
Hearts are merry, spirits bright.

Bundled together, stories unfold,
Memories made, both new and old.
Under the stars, wishes soar,
In this festive scene, we adore.

A Canvas of Stillness

White blankets cover the earth below,
Nature sleeps, wrapped in a glow.
Painting dreams with a silver brush,
The world holds still, in a hushed hush.

Flakes drift down without a sound,
A soft embrace, peace found.
Holiday lights begin to gleam,
Igniting hearts, like a warm dream.

In the stillness, laughter rings,
A rhythm found as joy sings.
Gathered close, love takes the stage,
In this moment, we turn a page.

With every twig and tree adorned,
In this season, we're reborn.
Celebration boundless, spirits rise,
Under the vast, wintry skies.

The Glow of Midnight

The clock strikes twelve, a moment bright,
The world awakens, filled with light.
Gathering sparks in gentle cheer,
Midnight magic, we're all here.

Starlit wishes begin to flow,
Hearts ablaze, like warm embers glow.
Champagne bubbles tickle the night,
In joyful chaos, spirits take flight.

Hands uplifted, voices raised,
In this moment, we are praised.
A chorus swells, ringing clear,
Together in love, we persevere.

As fireworks bloom against the sky,
Each burst of color, a jubilant cry.
With laughter echoing, we embrace,
This festive night, a warm, sweet grace.

Glacial Serenity

In the light of the winter sun,
Snowflakes dance, a twinkling fun.
Branches bear a lacy sheen,
Whispers of peace in the serene.

Children laugh, their joy in tow,
Building dreams in the soft, white glow.
A world wrapped in quiet delight,
As day melts into the gentle night.

Quietude Amidst the Flakes

A hush falls soft on the snowy ground,
Echoes of cheer in the stillness found.
Candles flicker, warm and bright,
Casting shadows, a festive sight.

Hot cocoa steams in the frosty air,
Hearts are full, laughter to share.
Wrapped in blankets, snug and warm,
Together we weather any storm.

Still Hearts

Softly they glide, the snowflakes fall,
Whispers of joy in the winter's call.
Golden lights twinkle through the trees,
Carols echo, carried on the breeze.

Gather 'round, let the stories unfold,
In the glow of the hearth, warmth to behold.
Friendships deepen, bonds arise,
In the stillness, love never dies.

The Softest Touch

Each touch of frost is a gentle kiss,
Nature's embrace, a moment of bliss.
Glowing fires spark in every home,
A tapestry woven, a place to roam.

Under the stars, spirits take flight,
Echoing joy in the magical night.
Together we share, hearts beating as one,
In this festive glow, our laughter's begun.

The Winter's Quilt

Snowflakes dance upon the ground,
Laughter echoes all around.
Children play with joyful cheer,
Winter's magic, drawing near.

Twinkling lights adorn the trees,
Whispers carried by the breeze.
Hot cocoa warms the chilly hands,
Together, dreaming of far lands.

Songs of old fill up the air,
Fireside talks and sweetened care.
Each moment wrapped in pure delight,
A quilted feel of cozy night.

Joyful hearts in harmony,
Celebrate in unity.
With every breath, pure love ignites,
This festive quilt, our hearts' delights.

Radiance in the Silence

In the stillness, lights aglow,
Gentle whispers, soft and slow.
Stars above in velvet skies,
Silent wishes, dreams that rise.

Candles flicker, shadows play,
Hope reflected in the gray.
Warmth of friendship fills the room,
In the silence, spirits bloom.

Laughter dances in the night,
Glowing faces, pure delight.
Each moment shared, a spark so bright,
Radiance found in soft moonlight.

As the world holds its breath tight,
We gather close in heart's pure light.
Together in this gentle grace,
Festive cheer, our warm embrace.

A Journey in White

Step by step in soft, wet snow,
Whispers of winter's ebb and flow.
Footprints lead to where we dream,
In this world, everything gleams.

Chasing shadows, laughter peals,
Through the woods, the silence heals.
Nature dons her sparkling dress,
A journey wrapped in pure finesse.

Friends united, mischief sparks,
Building castles, leaving marks.
Snowball fights and joyous shouts,
Warmth and love, that's what it's about.

Underneath the starlit sky,
Moments captured, sweet as pie.
With every breath, our hearts ignite,
In this journey, pure delight.

Calm beneath the Flakes

Gentle flurries start to fall,
Nature whispers, beckons all.
A blanket soft on earth's embrace,
Calm descends in winter's grace.

Branches heavy, laden low,
Sparkling jewels on tree and row.
Quiet moments, peace in sight,
Beneath the flakes, our spirits light.

Friends gather, sharing tales,
In the hush, our laughter sails.
Hearts entwined, a festive song,
Underneath where we belong.

In this calm, we find our cheer,
Together, holding loved ones near.
With every flake, a new delight,
Wrapped in joy, a pure respite.

Feathered Silence Across the Ground

Snowflakes dance in soft delight,
Whispers of a purest white.
Children cheer with laughter's sound,
Feathered silence wraps the ground.

Lights aglow in evening's charm,
Warmth of drinks, a cozy balm.
Yearning hearts in joyful cheer,
Gather close, the best time of year.

The Winter's Peaceful Palette

Brush of frost upon the trees,
Nature paints with gentle ease.
Scarves of color, bright and bold,
A festive tale in winter's hold.

Candles flicker, shadows play,
Joyous spirits come to stay.
Hot cocoa in each little hand,
Together we all take a stand.

Tranquil Threads of Crystal

Threads of crystal, softly spun,
Glistening under winter's sun.
A tapestry of snowflakes bright,
Harmony in purest white.

Frosty windows greet the night,
Whispers of warmth, hearts take flight.
Laughter mingles with the stars,
Together near, we've come so far.

Beneath the Thawing Sky

Beneath the thawing sky so wide,
Hope awakens, joy and pride.
Blossoms peek from sleeping ground,
A festive pulse in life is found.

Songs of warmth fill every space,
Time for love, a sweet embrace.
With each hug, the world does cheer,
In the magic, we find our sphere.

Lullaby of the Arctic

Soft winds whisper through the ice,
Dancing lights in the starry skies.
Snowflakes fall like dreams so bright,
Cradled in the arms of night.

Polar bears tread on frozen ground,
Nature's rhythm, a peaceful sound.
Children giggle in snow-clad play,
Winter's joy on this festive day.

Auroras flicker, a vibrant show,
Painting the landscape with winter's glow.
In this quiet, the heart finds cheer,
Embracing magic, the season near.

With each breath, the cold air sings,
A lullaby of the Arctic brings.
Together we share tales of delight,
In this realm of frost and light.

A Glimmer of Solitude

In the stillness of the frosty air,
Lies a glimmer both soft and rare.
Whispers dance on the frozen stream,
Echoing secrets of winter dreams.

A single star twinkles high above,
Not alone, but embraced with love.
Snowflakes twirl in their graceful flight,
As the world wraps itself in white.

Each breath draws in the chill so clear,
Yet in solitude, there's warmth, my dear.
The heart beats strong amid the cold,
In solitude, there's beauty untold.

Around the fire, we gather close,
Sharing stories that matter most.
In this quiet, our spirits soar,
With each moment, we ask for more.

Enchanted Chill

Through the woods, the snowflakes twirl,
Nature's magic begins to unfurl.
Underneath the moon's pale light,
There lies enchantment in the night.

Frosted branches, a wondrous sight,
Glowing softly, wrapped in white.
With every breath, the crisp air glints,
A tapestry of seasonal hints.

Laughter echoes beneath the trees,
Carried softly on the breeze.
Voices mingle with the chill,
Each moment crafted, time stands still.

As stars cascade in a velvety sky,
The world exhales a cozy sigh.
In this charm of winter's thrill,
We find ourselves in the enchanted chill.

The Truce of Winter

When winter comes with soft embrace,
A truce is made, a slower pace.
Blankets of white cloak every tree,
Inviting peace for you and me.

The crackle of fires, warmth within,
Whispers of joy, the calm begins.
With cocoa steaming, hearts aglow,
In winter's arms, we let love flow.

Footprints trace where dreams have strayed,
In frosted silence, laughter played.
Beneath the moon, we share our tales,
Of magic winds and friendly gales.

As soft snowflakes fall, we sway,
Together singing through the day.
In this truce, we find our way,
A festive spirit in winter's sway.

The Softest Touch of Quiet

In twilight's glow, the world sits still,
Soft whispers drift, a gentle thrill.
Bright lanterns flicker, shadows dance,
Laughter echoes, in a merry trance.

Snowflakes tumble, a frosty ballet,
As hearts unite in the joy of play.
Warm cocoa steams, with spice and cheer,
Embracing moments that draw us near.

Children giggle, in a playful chase,
With rosy cheeks, they find their place.
The night is young, with dreams in tow,
Beneath the stars' enchanting glow.

So let us freeze this time of glee,
Wrapped in warmth, just you and me.
The softest touch, a bond so true,
In this festive night, made just for two.

Winter's Muffled Melody

Whispers of winter weave through the night,
Stars above twinkle with pure delight.
Every breath dances, a chilly sigh,
As snowflakes gather, the world drifts by.

Candles flicker, casting golden beams,
In cozy corners, we share our dreams.
Voices rise in a jubilant song,
Echoes of laughter where we belong.

Snowmen stand proud in silvery white,
Hats and scarves make the scene just right.
Mittens embrace, as hands intertwine,
In moments of warmth, love's sweet design.

So let the melody softly play,
With hearts entwined, let's drift away.
Together we dance, in this winter's cheer,
Embracing joy that draws us near.

Silent Dances of the Frozen

Frozen landscapes, a quiet sigh,
Nature's stillness as time slips by.
Under the moon, the shadows glide,
Silent dances where dreams abide.

Branches adorned in sparkling frost,
In this wonderland, we've never lost.
Footsteps crunch on the powdery ground,
Where whispers of magic can still be found.

Stars twinkle like diamonds in the sky,
As laughter bubbles, passing by.
The cold air sparkles with joy and grace,
In this fleeting moment, we find our place.

So let's twirl in the chill of the night,
Wrapped in warmth, with hearts so light.
In silent dances, we craft our cheer,
In frozen whispers, love draws near.

A Lullaby in Flakes

Gentle snow falls, a lullaby sweet,
Covering the world in a soft retreat.
With each flake's touch, a tender embrace,
Winter's song wraps us in its grace.

Chimneys puff smoke, a warm delight,
Inviting us home on this cozy night.
Joyful carols fill the frosty air,
Echoing love that we all can share.

Twinkling lights adorn every street,
As neighbors gather, our hearts will meet.
With hands held tight, we revel and sway,
In laughter and stories, we find our way.

So let the snow fall, let it shine,
In this festive season, our spirits align.
A lullaby in flakes, warm as the sun,
Together we cherish, forever as one.

A Hushed Canvas of White

Snowflakes dance in the air,
Children's laughter fills the night.
Twinkling lights everywhere,
Hearts aglow, spirits bright.

Cocoa warms our frozen hands,
Carols echo through the trees.
Festive joy in many lands,
Hope and peace float on the breeze.

In the stillness, magic glows,
Every corner shines with cheer.
As the soft wind gently blows,
We share stories, love draws near.

Beneath the stars, we unite,
In this hushed, enchanted night.

Frost-kissed Moments of Reflection

Frosted branches, pure delight,
Memories wrapped in the glow.
Shared adventures through the night,
Each moment cherished, we know.

Gathered 'round, the fire's warm,
Laughter dances like the flame.
In this cozy, joyful charm,
Every heart beats just the same.

Snowflakes whisper soft and low,
Echoes of a time gone by.
In the stillness, feelings flow,
Underneath the frosty sky.

A festive pulse, we remember,
Frost-kissed dreams bring bright December.

Whispers of White

Gentle snow, a quiet song,
Covers earth like a white sheet.
Joyous crowds where we belong,
In the chill, our hearts still beat.

Candles flicker, shadows play,
Warming smiles and brightened eyes.
In the hush of winter's stay,
Hope and love can never die.

With each step, the world unfolds,
Footprints mark the path we tread.
In the laughter, life retolds,
Every word and joy we've spread.

Embrace the whispers of this night,
Under stars, everything feels right.

Tranquil Frost

Silent night, a soft embrace,
Trees adorned in glistening white.
Every breath a gentle grace,
In this wonder, pure delight.

Candied treats and joy abound,
Fingers wrapped 'round marshmallow.
In this love, we are all bound,
Hearts entwined in every glow.

Each moment holds a perfect cheer,
Dancing souls in winter's trance.
As the frosty air draws near,
We find magic in our dance.

Tranquil frost, our spirits soar,
In this festive night, we explore.

Silent Embrace

In the glow of twinkling lights,
Laughter fills the crisp, cool air.
Friends gather near, hearts warm and bright,
In this festive time that we share.

Joy dances softly on the breeze,
Sipping cocoa, feeling so blessed.
Snowflakes swirl, whispering with ease,
In a moment that feels like a quest.

Carols sung with a merry cheer,
Echoing through the starry night.
Wrapped in warmth, our bonds draw near,
In this silent embrace, pure delight.

As the clock chimes with gleeful sound,
Hope and love linger in the space.
Together, our hearts are unbound,
In this season, a silent embrace.

Shimmering Calm

Glistening stars adorn the sky,
Silent night holds a magic rare.
Underneath the moon's watchful eye,
Whispers of joy float in the air.

Candles flicker, casting soft glow,
Inviting warmth to every heart.
With every pause, tranquility flows,
In this calm, we find a fresh start.

Snowflakes dancing on every sigh,
Each one unique, a story told.
Happiness glimmers, lifting us high,
In this moment, a treasure to hold.

Songs of the season fill the air,
Harmonies weave a tapestry.
In the stillness, we breathe in prayer,
Finding peace in this shimmering calm.

Serene Flurries

Gentle flakes swirl and sway,
In a dance of silver delight.
Whispers of winter pave the way,
Softly falling, a mesmerizing sight.

Children laugh, their cheeks aglow,
Building dreams in the frosty white.
Joy cascades like a sparkling show,
In the heart of a starry night.

Fires crackle, warmth beckons near,
Muffled voices tell tales of old.
Gathered close, we hold each dear,
In serene flurries, warmth unfolds.

Drifting gently, the moments bless,
A canvas painted with holiday cheer.
Love and hope entwined in finesse,
In these serene flurries, we draw near.

Winter's Gentle Caress

Softly now, the snow descends,
Like a hush upon the ground.
A wonderland as the day ends,
In winter's arms, peace is found.

Festive lights begin to twinkle,
Reflecting joy in every heart.
With every laugh, our spirits crinkle,
Together, we'll never drift apart.

Mittens worn, we stroll outside,
Hand in hand, warmth so divine.
Beneath the stars, we take in stride,
In winter's gentle caress, we shine.

As voices mingle in sweet refrain,
And laughter echoes through the night.
In our memories, love will remain,
Holding tight to winter's gentle light.

Frosted Horizons

Morning breaks with sparkling light,
Frosty fields gleam, pure and bright.
Laughter echoes in the air,
Joy and warmth beyond compare.

Families gather, smiles abound,
In every heart, love is found.
Children's giggles fill the scene,
In this moment, all is serene.

Snowflakes dance in swirling flight,
While we bask in winter's delight.
Bonfires crackle, stories flow,
In the glow of hearth's warm glow.

As day fades into twilight's grace,
With every moment, we embrace.
Frosted horizons stretch so wide,
In festive spirits, we take pride.

The Dance of the Winter Wind

Whispers of the breeze around,
Winter's song is sweetly found.
Footprints trail on frosty ground,
As hearts and laughter gather round.

Mittens worn and cheeks aglow,
Joyful spirits start to flow.
Skaters glide on icy lakes,
With every twirl, the cold heart wakes.

Cups of cocoa steaming high,
Underneath the starlit sky.
Families toast with cheer divine,
In this winter, all align.

The night unfolds, a shining dance,
With every twirl, we take our chance.
Winter wind, a gentle guide,
In this festive night, we confide.

Delicate Balance

In the stillness, peace descends,
Nature's beauty never ends.
Snowflakes fall like whispered dreams,
Glistening soft in moonlit beams.

Colors bloom beneath the frost,
In every breath, we find what's lost.
Candles flicker, hearts entwine,
In this moment, love's divine.

Joyful songs fill the cool night air,
Memories linger, beyond compare.
Hand in hand, we wander free,
In the dance of harmony.

The balance of the season's grace,
Wrapped in warmth, a sweet embrace.
Each heartbeat echoes, pure and bright,
In this festive, wondrous night.

Twilight in White

As daylight fades, a hush for all,
Twilight whispers, night will call.
Snow blankets softly, pure and light,
Under stars that shimmer bright.

Gathered close by candle's glow,
We share our dreams, our hearts bestow.
Songs of joy weave through the night,
In every note, we feel the light.

With every cheer, the air turns sweet,
Footsteps dance in rhythmic beat.
Voices rise in joyous cheer,
Winter magic drawing near.

Twilight in white, a stunning sight,
In festivities, hearts unite.
As we celebrate, love ignites,
In this season, pure delights.

Murmurs of the Frozen

Whispers of joy in the icy air,
Laughter and songs, hearts full of cheer.
Sparkling snowflakes dance and sway,
Under bright stars, night turns to day.

Firelight flickers, warm and bright,
Friends gathered close, a beautiful sight.
With cozy blankets, we share our dreams,
In this frosty world, nothing's as it seems.

Every twinkle of lights, a story told,
Of love and magic, worth more than gold.
Murmurs of hope in the winter chill,
Festive moments, the heart's sweet thrill.

So raise a glass to the moonlit night,
To memories forged in pure delight.
In the embrace of friends so dear,
Life's greatest treasures, gathered here.

Stillness Beneath the Drift

Silence blankets, soft as a sigh,
As snowflakes fall from the starlit sky.
Nature's lullaby whispers so sweet,
In this stillness, our hearts softly beat.

Children bundled, making snowmen,
Smiling faces, joy without end.
Frost-kissed branches, a delicate frame,
In the winter's arms, we feel the same.

Candles flicker, casting warm glow,
While outside, the chilly winds blow.
With cocoa steaming, we gather near,
Sharing our stories, holding them dear.

The night is alive with holiday cheer,
In this frozen wonder, love draws near.
Together we cherish this time of rest,
Finding true bliss in moments the best.

Gentle Grace of Winter

First light dawns with a soft embrace,
The world adorned in winter's grace.
Every branch a work of art,
Nature's canvas, a joyful heart.

We stroll through paths where shadows play,
Footsteps crunch in a frosty ballet.
Laughter rings out, a melody clear,
In winter wonder, we hold dear.

Each hot drink warms our fingers tight,
As golden rays chase away the night.
Friendship's glow in the gentle chill,
A festive spirit, a tranquil thrill.

So let us dance beneath the trees,
In the crisp air that sings with ease.
Wrapped in moments, boundless and free,
The gentle grace of winter, we see.

Whispers of Winter

Snowflakes dance through the air,
Laughter echoes, hearts aware.
Lights aglow on branches high,
Winter's secret, oh so nigh.

Children bundled, spirits bright,
Gifts exchanged in soft twilight.
Warmth of cocoa in our hands,
Joy and love, our hearts expand.

Crisp air filled with songs of cheer,
Moments shared, each one sincere.
Cozy firesides, stories told,
In the chill, we find pure gold.

As the stars begin to gleam,
We embrace this wondrous dream.
With each whisper of the night,
Festive magic takes its flight.

A Blanket of Calm

Gentle snow drapes o'er the ground,
Silence reigns, a sacred sound.
Footprints soft where children tread,
In this peace, our worries shed.

Candles flicker, shadows play,
Gathered 'round, we greet the day.
Comfort found in every face,
In this warmth, we find our place.

Mugs of cheer, the laughter flows,
Tales of joy, the friendship grows.
Harmony in every breath,
This blanket wraps us, even Death.

With each moment, hearts align,
A gentle touch, so pure, divine.
Embraced by winter's soft embrace,
In calm stillness, we find grace.

Tranquility Unveiled

Underneath the silver moon,
Winter's peace arrives too soon.
Branches whisper, secrets shared,
In this tranquil scene, we're spared.

Softly falling, snowflakes gleam,
In our hearts, a gentle dream.
Every breath a fleeting sigh,
As the world slows down to lie.

Laughter lingers, bonds we forge,
Around the fire, warmth we gorge.
Golden embers flicker bright,
In the stillness, pure delight.

With the night, our spirits soar,
In this calm, we yearn for more.
Tranquility, a gift to hold,
Wrapped in winter, dreams unfold.

The Harmony of Hues

Colors burst in festive cheer,
Every shade, the heart draws near.
Ornaments glisten, spirits rise,
Underneath the winter skies.

Red and green in joyful blend,
Strangers meet, and friendships mend.
Songs of hope and laughter flow,
In this harmony, love will grow.

Candied treats and warm delights,
Celebrate these festive nights.
Every smile, a spark of light,
In the dark, we shine so bright.

With each hue, a story spun,
Shared with all, we laugh and run.
In this wonderland, we play,
The harmony of hues, our way.

Reflections in the Snow

Sparkling crystals dance in light,
Laughter echoes through the night.
Children play, their voices cheer,
Winter's magic, ever near.

Tracks of joy in white so pure,
Footprints left, of love secure.
Hot cocoa brews by the fire,
Hearts ignite with warm desire.

Stars above like diamonds glow,
Whispers of the fallen snow.
Time to share, to hold so tight,
Festive dreams take joyful flight.

As the world in stillness rests,
Love surrounds, and every quest.
Beneath the moon, a gentle sigh,
In snowy realms, our spirits fly.

The Pause of Nature

In the hush of winter's breath,
Nature wraps its joy in depth.
Branches draped in glistening lace,
Whispers of a sacred space.

Stars above in harmony,
Dancing softly, wild and free.
Silent night, a gentle pause,
Nature's wonder earns applause.

Each heartbeat echoes crisp and clear,
A collection of all we hold dear.
Gather 'round, let stories blend,
In this magic, hearts extend.

With every flake, a gentle kiss,
In winter's arms, there is bliss.
Embrace the warmth, let spirits soar,
In nature's pause, we long for more.

Calm after the Flurry

The storm has danced its wild display,
Now peace wraps the world in grey.
Softly fallen, blankets white,
Hints of joy in pure delight.

Branches bow with heavy grace,
Nature sighs, finds its place.
Children whisper, soft and low,
Calm has come after the snow.

Hot fires crackle, warmth to share,
Laughter dances through the air.
As candles flicker, shadows play,
Hearts unite, come what may.

Outside the world, a crystal scheme,
Inside our hearts, a golden dream.
Together we found peace anew,
In the calm, friendships grew.

Gentle Transformation

The world awakens, draped in white,
A festive canvas, pure delight.
Icicles shimmer, catching light,
Transformations in the night.

Crisp air sings of joy and cheer,
Gathering loved ones, holding near.
Warmth of spirit softly glows,
In every heart, the magic flows.

Lights adorn the trees with grace,
Every shadow finds its place.
Songs of old, we sing anew,
In this moment, love breaks through.

As winter's charm begins to show,
We dance and twirl in gentle flow.
Life transforms in colors bright,
In every heart, a spark ignites.

Shadows in the Slumbering Snow

Beneath the moon's soft, silver glow,
The whispers dance in gentle flow.
Snowflakes twinkle, pure and bright,
As shadows play in the soft twilight.

Laughter echoes through the trees,
Carried softly on the breeze.
Children's joy in a frosty flight,
Painting dreams of pure delight.

Warm embers crackle, fires glow,
In cozy nooks, we share the show.
Stories woven with every cheer,
As holiday magic draws us near.

In the silent night, we find our peace,
In frosty air, our hearts release.
Together wrapped in winter's glee,
Shadows drift, our spirits free.

Embracing the Frosty Stillness

A crystal veil adorns the land,
Wrapped in beauty, soft and grand.
The world is hushed, the stars align,
Under winter's gentle design.

Each breath we take, a cloud of white,
As joy ignites this frosty night.
Hands entwined amidst the chill,
Hearts grow warm, our laughter spills.

The air is sweet with spicy cheer,
As mugs of cider bring us near.
Festive lights in colors bright,
Illuminate this winter night.

In a quilt of warmth, we find our place,
With glowing smiles on every face.
Embracing stillness, side by side,
In frosty wonder, we abide.

Echoes of the Icy Breeze

Whispers travel on the icy air,
Through barren branches, everywhere.
A symphony of winter's call,
Echoes softly, a festive thrall.

In the distance, sleigh bells chime,
Bringing magic, a dance in time.
Children rush to greet the snow,
With cheeks aglow, their joy will grow.

The world adorned in brilliant white,
Each twinkling star, a guiding light.
Echoes of laughter fill the eve,
As hearts awaken, we believe.

Together in this frosty spell,
We weave our dreams, a tale to tell.
Echoes of the icy breeze,
A bond of love, our spirits ease.

A Tapestry of Chilled Dreams

A canvas spread of snowy white,
We paint our hopes in purest light.
Every flake, a wish unfurled,
In this enchanted, sparkling world.

Stars above, like diamonds gleam,
As we pursue our frosty dream.
Warmed by laughter, hand in hand,
Together in this winter land.

The twilight hums a cheerful tune,
Beneath the watchful, glowing moon.
A tapestry of frosty schemes,
Woven tight in chilled dreams.

With every hug, a cozy blend,
The beauty of this night won't end.
In this wonder, let us stay,
As festive joys light up the way.

Whispers of Winter's Embrace

Snowflakes dance in the evening light,
Joyous laughter fills the air bright.
Warmth of fires, their flicker and glow,
A festive spirit begins to flow.

Gathered friends in hats and scarves,
With mugs of cocoa, we share our laughs.
Twinkling lights on every bough,
In winter's charm, we take a vow.

Songs of joy echo through the night,
Hearts unite in the soft moonlight.
With every cheer, the chill retreats,
In winter's hush, our love repeats.

A season of magic, both young and old,
Stories unfolding, in warmth we hold.
Together, we weave a tapestry bright,
In whispers of winter, pure delight.

Tranquil Blankets of White

Softly drifting down from above,
Nature wraps us in a blanket of love.
Each flake a whisper, unique and rare,
In tranquil beauty, we find our share.

Trees wear coats of glistening white,
As stars emerge, filling the night.
Harmonies of silence, crisp and clear,
In this sweet season, we hold so dear.

Children bundled in vibrant hues,
Building dreams beneath the blues.
Snowmen grinning with buttons and charms,
In tranquil blankets, we find our arms.

Fires crackle with a gentle sway,
Hearts are warmed in a snowy ballet.
Together we cherish this special sight,
In tranquil blankets, pure delight.

Hushed Elegance Descends

In the stillness, a soft descant,
Winter whispers with a gentle chant.
Lace-like fingers brush the trees,
A hushed elegance, where all can freeze.

Golden glows from the windows shine,
Inviting warmth, where hearts align.
In every corner, laughter gleams,
As joy unravels like delicate dreams.

With frosted steps on the polished snow,
We glide and twirl, letting spirits flow.
Beneath the stars, a secret unfolds,
In hushed elegance, our wonder beholds.

Gathered together, the night feels bright,
In cozy moments, we bask in light.
With every heartbeat, memories blend,
In hushed elegance, love's message we send.

Frosted Serenity

Morning dawns with a frosted hue,
Nature whispers secrets, fresh and new.
With glistening paths that beckon us near,
In frosted serenity, there's nothing to fear.

Soft sighs of winter, a gentle embrace,
In every corner, a magical space.
Icicles glisten like diamonds at dawn,
In nature's canvas, wonder is drawn.

Crisp air carries the scent of pine,
Guiding our hearts as our spirits entwine.
In serene moments, we pause and reflect,
In frosted serenity, we find our perfect.

With festive cheer that twinkles and glows,
A tapestry of warmth, as the cool wind blows.
Together we cherish this season's song,
In frosted serenity, we all belong.

www.ingramcontent.com/pod-product-compliance
Ingram Content Group UK Ltd.
Pitfield, Milton Keynes, MK11 3LW, UK
UKHW030853221224
452712UK00006B/243